The Adventures of Roger The Chicken

Colour and Create Your Own Adventures

Author Glenn Cox
Illustrator Fenny Fu

Copyright © 2020 Glenn Cox

Written by Glenn Cox

Illustrations by Mikucchi

The purchase of this colouring book grants you the right to photocopy the contents for home and classroom use. Copy permission is for private or church use.

All other rights reserved. No part of this publication may be reproduced, distributed, or transmitted in any form or by any means other commercial use or for financial gain, without the prior written permission of the author.

ISBN-13: 978-0987460776

A note to you from me

I hope you enjoy colouring in *The Adventures of Roger the Chicken*. This has been fun to see my children colour in these pictures. And I have a surprise for you!!! You can learn how to draw Roger the Chicken and Barry the Duck. Then you can draw Roger and Barry onto the pictures at the end of the book. Add in your own little stories of Roger and Barry having fun on the farm. I would love to see them. Please post them to our Facebook page "The Adventures of Roger the Chicken".

A quick thought while you are colouring in.

Ephesians 2:10 - *For we are God's masterpiece. He has created us anew in Christ Jesus, so we can do the good things he planned for us long ago. (NLT © 1996, 2004, 2015)*

WHEN YOU THINK OF A MASTERPIECE WHAT DO YOU THINK OF? DO YOU THINK OF AN AMAZING PICTURE OF A TREE BESIDE A BEAUTIFUL STREAM THAT SOMEONE HAS DRAWN? OR A BEAUTIFUL PHOTO OF A SUNSET ACROSS AN OCEAN? WITH COLOURS OF PINK AND BLUE AND PURPLE COLOURING THE SAND AND THE OCEAN? A PHOTO OF GOD'S CREATIVE ABILITY.

BUT GOD'S MOST CREATIVE MASTERPIECE IS YOU! FOR YOU ARE GOD'S MASTERPIECE! HE CREATED YOU TO DO GOOD THINGS. DID YOU KNOW GOD CREATED YOU UNIQUELY? HE CREATED YOU TO ADD TO HIS BEAUTIFUL DESIGN. HE CREATED YOU TO ADD COLOUR TO THE PEOPLE AROUND YOU. LIKE IF YOU HELP YOUR PARENTS, MAYBE YOUR ADDING A STROKE OF BLUE THAT FADES INTO PINK. OR SPEAKING KINDLY TO YOUR BROTHER OR SISTER. OR FORGIVING YOUR FRIEND – MMM, WHAT COLOUR MIGHT YOU BE ADDING?

YOU ARE GOD'S MASTERPIECE. HE CREATED YOU TO BE CREATIVE. SO COLOUR WHEREVER YOU ARE BY DOING GOOD THINGS.

How to Draw Roger the Chicken

How to Draw Barry the Duck

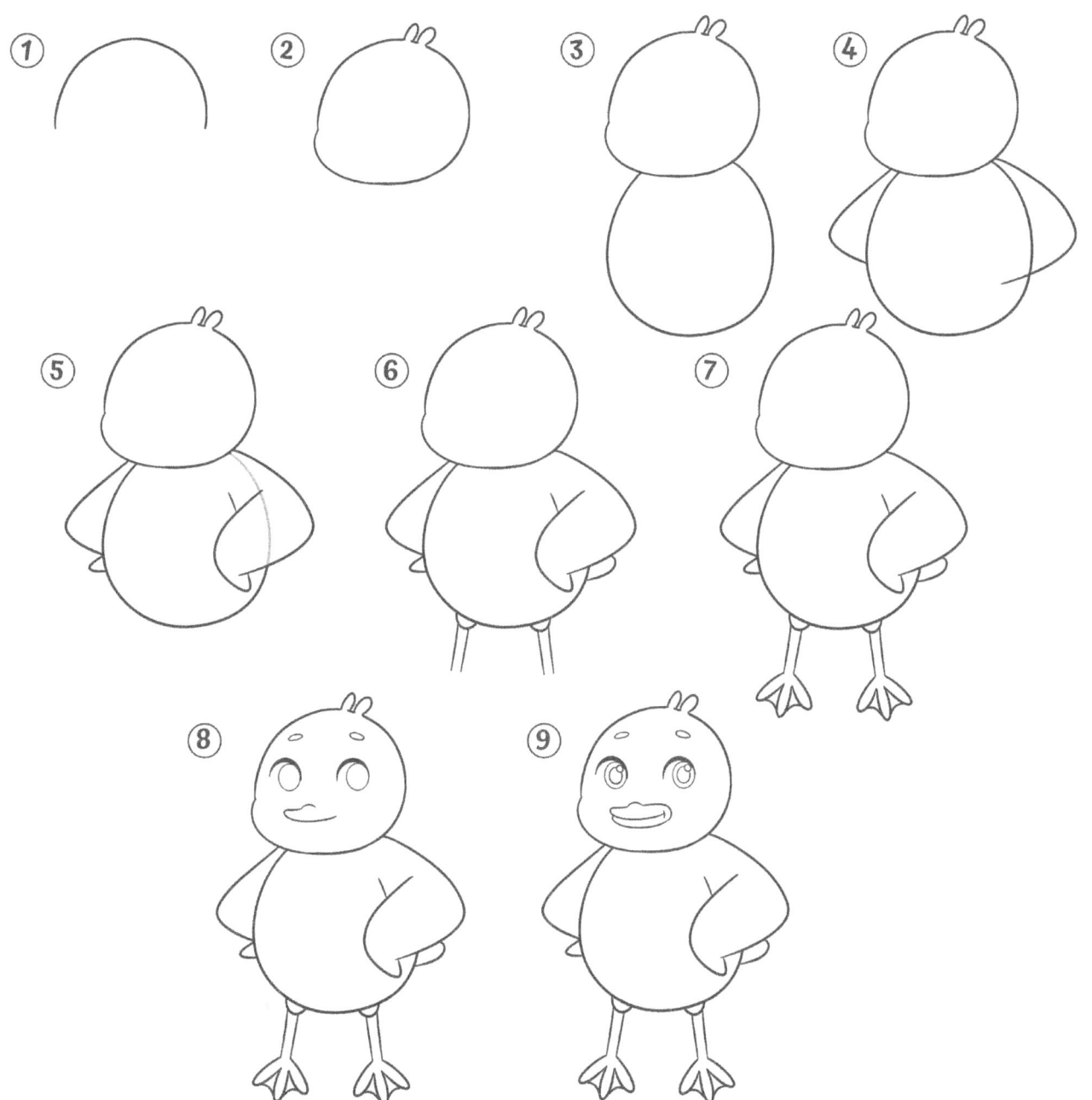

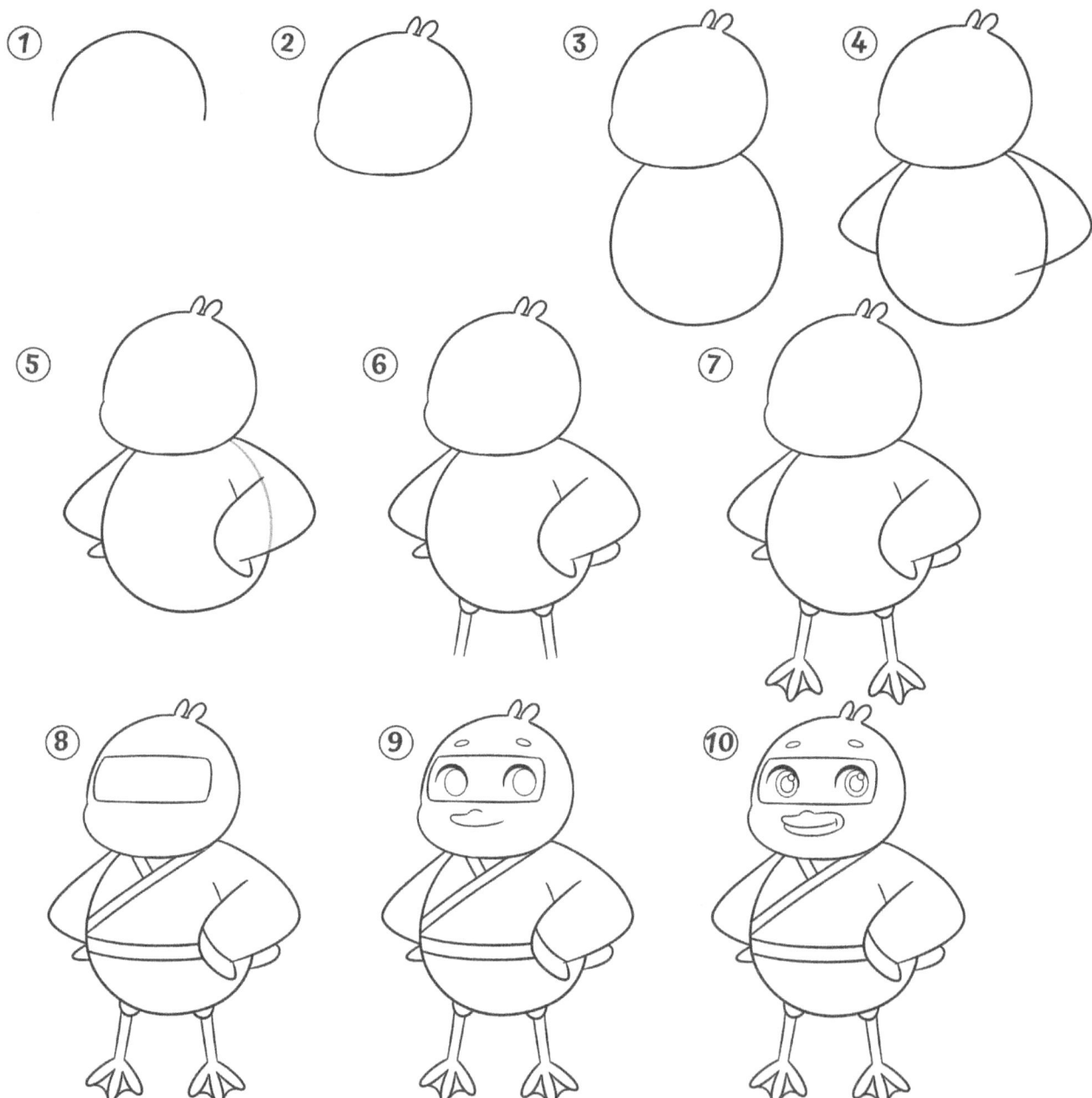

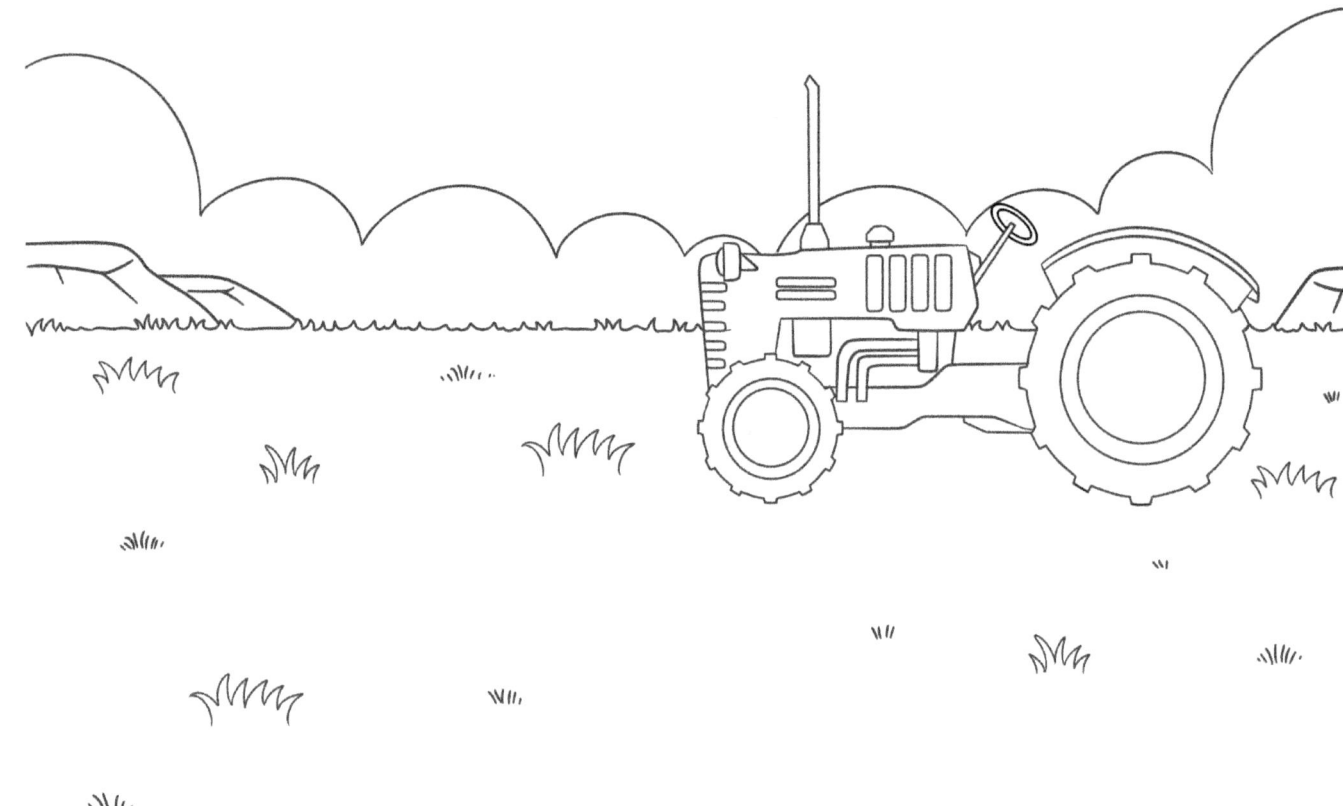

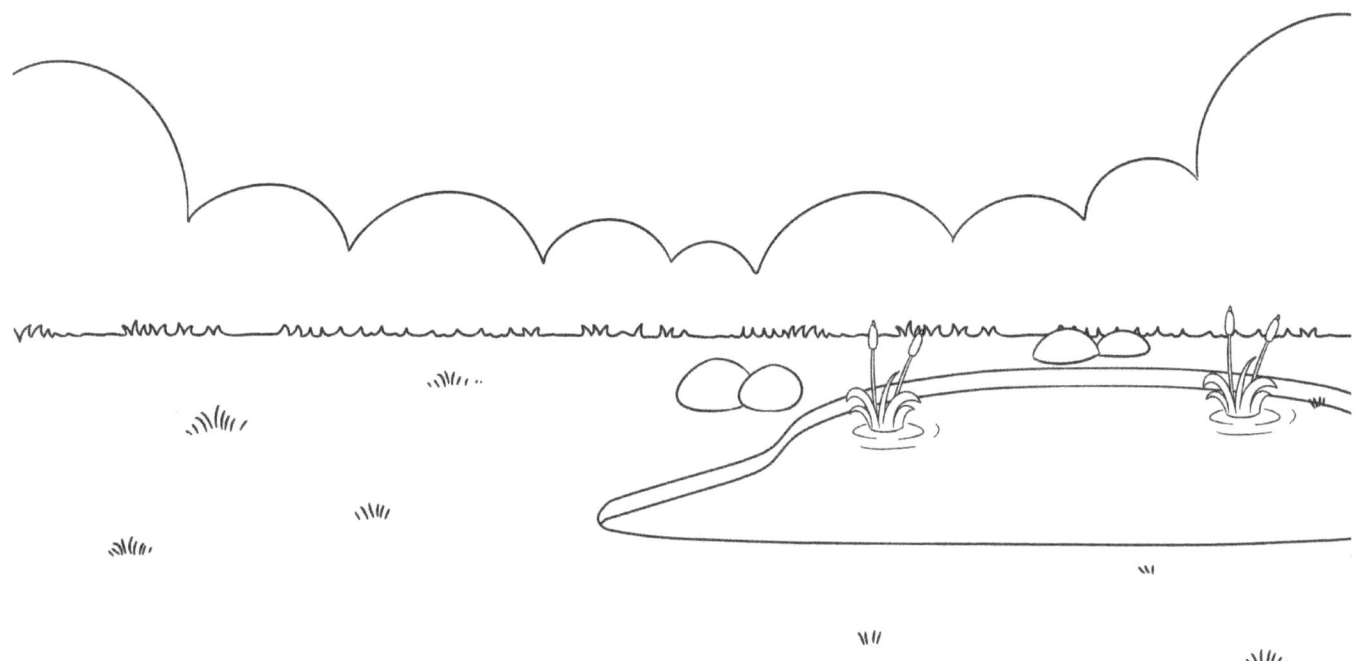

www.ingramcontent.com/pod-product-compliance
Lightning Source LLC
Chambersburg PA
CBHW080126020526
44112CB00036B/2746